Everyday Talk
about
Sex and Marriage

Everyday Talk about Sex and Marriage

A BIBLICAL HANDBOOK FOR PARENTS

JOHN A. YOUNTS
WITH DAVID YOUNTS

Foreword by Kirk Cameron

Everyday Talk about Sex and Marriage

© 2017 John A. Younts with David Younts

ISBN:
Print: 978-1-63342-087-8
ePub: 978-1-63342-088-5
Mobi: 978-1-63342-089-2

Published by **Shepherd Press**
P.O. Box 24
Wapwallopen, PA 18660

www.shepherdpress.com

BE   25   24   23   22   21   20   19   18   17
     14   13   12   11   10   9   8   7   6   5   4   3   2   1

Library of Congress Cataloging-in-Publication Data

Designed by **documen**

CONTENTS

As a dad of six quickly growing children, I'm feeling that pressing but awkward responsibility more each day: I know I need to have "The Talk" with my boys and my girls—and before they are educated about it by friends, movies, music, and the internet. I think I can do a much better job than any of these lesser teachers. Also, I know that God has positioned me perfectly, as a parent, to prepare these future moms and dads within my home. My biggest challenge is, of course, that I didn't have "the talk" I wish I'd had with my parents. The whole subject is one I'd rather not have to bring up with my kids either, due to its challenges and awkwardness. But, hey, if the birds and the bees understand it, and dogs and cows aren't embarrassed to show public displays of affection in parks and on farms, then there must be a way to present the information to my children in an engaging, beautiful, inspiring, and relational way. I think I have found my start here, in Jay's fresh new approach to the subject.

I have read some authors who talk about sex and marriage (and the perversions of both) in a way that either downgrades sex into irreverence, crudity, vulgarity, and the pompous pursuit of personal pleasure, or is too mechanical and clinical, downplaying the exciting passion and romantic story that every young man and woman wants to be a part of. Some authors have even succeeded in convincing their audience that "knowing your spouse" is just a necessary evil of producing offspring. The bedroom is approached with a hyper-religious attitude of, "Lord, if there is any way this cup can pass from me... but nevertheless, not my will, but thine be done." Yikes!

Marriage and sex are bound together and embedded in the original garden story of the first Superman (Adam: the once-sinless Prince of God) and his perfectly beautiful companion. Together they ruled the world and had the hope of anything their eyes could see and their hearts could imagine. Also, they were given more than one mode to express their desire and care for one another: words and works. Language and love. Sentence and sex. Both kinds of interaction produce deep knowledge between the two who become one flesh. In fact, in the beginning, God made one man. Then, declaring it was not good for him to be alone, God broke the one man into two (removed a rib) and created Eve. Then, girl meets boy—and the two become one again. One becomes two. Two become one. And the "one-ness" is seen most clearly in the birth of the new creatures made in the couple's image. These image-bearers are the glorious gifts that come from heaven to bless the world with the knowledge of God as they push the boundaries of the garden paradise to the edges of the earth. The maturation of the kingdom cannot be done in one generation. It takes children. Lots of them. Good ones. Godly ones. And ones who themselves will love having lots of children to continue the Great Assignment of Heaven-izing the world.

I appreciate Jay's fresh perspective, particularly the conversations between parent and child. These conversations help me, not only to see how I myself can view the subject, but also to hear what it might sound like when I do talk with my kids. This book has enriched my own understanding of the glory of marriage and all of its accompanying blessings. The underlying principles of the teaching you are about to read are profoundly biblical, dazzlingly insightful, and fun to read. After completing each chapter and its real world conversation, I couldn't wait to get to the next chapter to see how these interrelated concepts came together to paint a full and rich picture, for me and my children, of God's goodness and of his extravagant gift of marriage and sex. Enjoy!

Kirk Cameron

This book is divided into two parts. The first part contains the biblical basis and application for talking with your children about marriage and sex. We will look at specific passages and then make application of these passages as they relate to current culture issues of our day.

The second part contains examples of conversation starters. These sample conversations are not necessarily meant to be a word-for-word guide. Rather they are intended to provide ideas about what to include when you do have these conversations and to anticipate how your teenagers might respond to certain topics. Use them as sort of a test run to prepare for the real thing!

I am thankful to God for the blessing of working with my son David on this project and for the encouragement of my friend, Kirk Cameron. I also want to express my gratitude to Tim Challies for originally suggesting I do a series of blog posts on this topic! And I continue to be grateful for the love, guidance and support of my wife Ruth. My writing would never have happened without her passion for God's truth, her vision, literary skill, and commitment to me.

Our prayer is that God will bless you as you work through these important topics with your children.

John A. Younts with David Younts

PART 1

1

Talking to Your Children about Sex and Marriage

One of the more challenging of parental responsibilities is telling children about sex. This conversation is often so awkward that both parent and child wonder what good could come from it. Sometimes, there is no actual conversation. A parent might hand a book to his or her child and say, "Read this and let me know if you have any questions." There is a degree of irony in this awkwardness. On the one hand, it is almost impossible to avoid being confronted with sex. Movies, billboards, commercials, songs, news reports, casual conversations, TV programs etc., form a cultural bombardment of sexual themes that invade daily life. On the other hand, at least in most Christian households, sex is not talked about as a part of regular family conversation. So as soon as your children have unsupervised access to the world outside your home, they will begin to hear of affairs, gays, oral sex, people being "hot," people being "turned on," masturbation, and any number of references to sexual activity, ranging from subtle to crude. So what is not talked about at home is encountered with regularity outside the home. The reality is that your children will likely hear about sexual activity and sexual perversion long before you actually sit down to talk with them about what sex is. You know this and your children know this. As I said—it's awkward.

This awkwardness has come about because the world and, unfortunately, most Christians view sex in the same way. The world views sex as something distinct from marriage. In the world's thinking, marriage is a place where sex may occur, but marriage is not necessary for sex. There are few restrictions in modern Western culture on when, where and with whom sexual activity may take place. Restricting sex to marriage is at best a well-meaning but archaic religious tradition that is simply a denial of basic human nature and needs. Most discussions about sexuality outside the home focus on having sex that is pleasurable and safe. This view is the perspective embraced by advocates of sex education in our school systems. Masturbation, homosexual sex, and straight sex are all appropriate. This is the inevitable outcome when marriage and sex become separated from each other. The truth is that God designed sex for the setting of marriage alone. This is where the discussion about sex must begin.

This point may not seem to be important, but it is. Sex and marriage must be discussed together. Let's look at Genesis 1:28 and 2:24:

> *And God blessed them. And God said to them,*
> *"Be fruitful and multiply and fill the earth and*
> *subdue it and have dominion over the fish of the*
> *sea and over the birds of the heavens and over*
> *every living thing that moves on the earth."*
> *Therefore a man shall leave his father and his*
> *mother and hold fast to his wife, and they shall*
> *become one flesh.*

When asked about divorce, Jesus Christ put these two passages together to define what marriage is.

> *"Haven't you read," he replied, "that at the beginning the Creator 'made them male and female,' and said, 'For this reason a man will leave his father and mother and be united to his wife, and the two will become one flesh'? So they are no longer two, but one. Therefore what God has joined together, let man not separate."*
>
> (Matthew 19:4-6)

God made man male and female. He gave them the directive to have children, to fill, subdue, and rule the earth for his pleasure. The call to be fruitful and multiply is specifically tied to marriage in Genesis 2:24 and in Jesus' commentary on this same passage. This relationship of husbands and wives is consummated when they become one flesh as a result of their union. Pre-Fall this meant that in marriage men and women were to be united as one flesh to carry out God's mission of having dominion over the earth for God's glory. In the perfect sinless world before the Fall, this calling could mean nothing less. This is further underscored by Paul's quotation of this same passage in Ephesians 5. Here Paul likens this one flesh relationship between husband and wife to the relationship between Christ and his church.

This, then, is where you must start in teaching your children about sex. Sex is not fundamentally a biological, physiological activity. Sexuality is a necessary aspect of God's purpose for man to occupy and control the earth for the glory of God. All of the physiological phenomena that happens to the human body while engaging in sexual activity is expressly designed by God to remind husbands and wives that they have been called to unity, intimacy and procreation in their mission to have dominion over the earth. Sexual activity is designed for a man and a woman who are obeying God in marriage in order to bring honor to his name. The idea that sexual pleasure is designed merely and primarily for self-interest is pagan at its core. It is dishonoring to God to talk about sex in abstraction from marriage. The whole of the Christian life, in fact, is focused on the sacrificial and selfless love of others done in imitation of Christ according to 1 John 4:7-12. Sex cannot be both God-honoring and self-serving. Sex is specifically designed for marriage and for nothing else.

This principle means that you want to lay the proper foundation for talking about marriage and sex with your children. This will provide a more natural transition when you talk with your children about the specifics. In this context we will address:

- When to talk about sex
- What specifics should be covered at what age
- What sexual attraction is
- Abuses of God's provision for sexual activity

In some ways, these topics should be a part of your everyday talk as parents, but there is still the appropriateness of having a specific discussion when the time is right. I wanted to lay this foundation first: marriage and sex go together. This one parameter will help you to present biblical sexuality in a way that honors God and blesses your children.

2

When to Talk about Sex and Marriage

It is vital to keep sex and marriage linked because that is how the Bible presents them. Sex is not designed or intended for self-pleasure. Sex does bring pleasure, but engaging in sex for the primary purpose of fulfilling personal desires is the gateway to lust. As Ephesians 4:17-19 teaches, sensitivity to others (the biblical motivation for sex) is the opposite of sensuality (the self-serving pursuit of pleasure). Sensuality leads to sexual perversion and to God's harsh judgment of abandoning people to their own desires, condemning them to the ultimate consequences of their desires (Romans 1:18-32). Thus, when you teach your young children to prefer others above themselves and to find joy in sharing their toys and time, you are already preparing them to enjoy and honor God in marriage and sexual relationships.

One significant responsibility of being a biblical parent is to anticipate the temptations and struggles that your children will face in life. Talk about sexual themes has become part of our cultural landscape. In 2010, USA Today ran this story on sex and television on its website. Note the opening lines of the story:

"If sex sells, TV programmers are adding inventory to an already humongous sale.

Viewers are about to see full-frontal male nudity, heterosexual, homosexual and group sex, and graphic scenes rarely—if ever—seen on mainstream TV."

Sadly, what was predicted is coming true.

While you may be carefully screening your children's viewing habits, you can be confident that the images predicted in this article will be seen and talked about by children that your children interact with. This cultural context means that you will need to talk with your children about sex and marriage earlier rather than later. The USA Today article exemplifies the cultural, pagan view of separating sex from marriage. This view is one that you need to counter early on. Here is an excerpt from my book, *Everyday Talk* (page 113), that addresses this timing issue:

> You don't have to begin talking about sex the way the world does. Graphic content and biological illustrations are not profitable for discussion about sex with your very young children. It is better to keep it simple and conceptual in the beginning. Tell them something like this:
>
> Sex is something special that God created for married people. It is a way for mommies and daddies to be close and special with each other. Sex is a blessing because it is designed to help husbands and wives know each other and bring joy to each other. Sex is also how God makes babies grow inside of mommies. But, sometimes people who aren't married want to be close like that, and that is bad.

Initially that is all that you need to say. Learn how to communicate these thoughts to your children in your own words.

The idea is to build on this theme as your children grow older. It is not difficult to imagine a seven-year-old asking, "Mommy, what is a hooking up?" or "What does living together mean?" At that age, it is not helpful to enter into a discussion about the physical aspects of sexuality. Rather, you could say that it is a type of behavior that is disobedient to God because people who are not married are attempting to find pleasure in ways that he has forbidden. Since sex is designed for a man and a woman who are married, it is therefore wrong for people who are not husband and wife to engage in sexual activity. You can tell your seven-year-old that you will explain more to him as he matures, but that for now, this is what he needs to know. Sexual behavior of any type is reserved by God for marriage.

The important concept to grasp is that talk about sex and marriage will have to be updated incrementally, rather than having one comprehensive discussion at a time just before puberty. You should still have a major discussion about marriage and sex, but there should be many preliminary ones leading up to it. That is different from the more traditional way many of us expect this conversation to happen. However, the overtly sexual nature of our culture demands this more intentional, purposeful approach. One consequence of the church failing to be salt and light is that our culture is increasingly buying into a shameless, pagan view of sexuality.

USA Today also ran this article in its print version. This scenario is not impossible to imagine – your ten-year-old son picks up a copy of the paper that your husband left on the kitchen table. He got the paper on his recent business trip; he didn't have time to read the paper, but thought that others in the family might want to look at the paper. Your son finds the front page article on sex and TV and reads the opening lines that I copied above. You are not present when he glanced at the article. Try to put yourself in his place. Nudity, group sex, etc., on mainstream TV – temptation has arrived. Your son needs a game plan about how to handle this information in a way that pleases God and protects him. This situation is exactly what Proverbs 6:20-24 envisions when it describes what godly parental instruction should accomplish for your children. Here is what verse 22 says:

When you walk, their counsel will lead you.
When you sleep, they will protect you.
When you wake up, they will advise you.

Your son needs to have the godly counsel of his parents' wise instruction leading him as he reads the words of the article in USA Today. Chapter 7 in Proverbs then gives a concrete example of how this instruction can provide counsel. The father in chapter 7 sees a brazen wife leading a foolish young man into adultery. Instead of closing the curtain and diverting his son's attention from the unfolding drama outside their window, this father calls his son over and provides a running, specific commentary on what is taking place. This father knows that one day a woman like this will confront his son with the wicked, but tempting, offer of sexual pleasure apart from marriage. So he prepared his son for what he would someday face. This kind of instruction can become life-saving counsel.

The point here is to realize that your children will be confronted with the opportunity for sexual activity and thoughts long before you are comfortable talking about these things. In this situation, if you have followed the example of Proverbs 6:22 and chapter 7, your ten year-old son will have already heard from you that this kind of thing is becoming more prevalent in our culture. He will have already heard that this culture is engaged in a sensual pursuit of sexual pleasure outside of marriage. (This scenario applies equally to daughters.) Again, you can avoid some of the graphic details with younger children by saying that the activities referred to in the article are all against what God has commanded. But children ten and older will need something more specific. You can reference affectionate embraces, kissing, and warm physical contact between folks that are married as things that God has reserved for marriage. For example, it is a good thing for Mom and Dad to kiss each other, but not a good thing if they kiss people they are not married to. You can explain that this sort of physical interaction leads to more intimate sexual activity that is appropriate only for married people to have. When the world offers passionate kissing and related activities as normal for people who are not married, a trap is being laid similar to the one described in Proverbs 7. Yes, sexual activity is pleasurable; that is why it is tempting. Stress to your children that sex outside of marriage is selfish and destructive, even though at first it may appear to be rewarding and beneficial. That is the line of temptation used by the adulterous wife in Proverbs 7. However, the heart ruled by faith rather than sensuality believes God's Words are truth rather than believing the lies of sexual temptation.

This kind of in-the-trenches battle against the wave of sexual temptation is one for which you must prepare your children. By placing sexual activity in the context of marriage, you can more naturally engage your children about the deceptive allure of sex outside of marriage. In one sense, "the talk" about sexuality should be an ongoing, expanding one. However, you still must have a time when you prepare your prepubescent children for the changes that will occur in their bodies and in their own thinking. Exactly when that talk should happen will be different for each child—but make it your business to have that talk before puberty begins.

Next we will look at what to say when you do talk with your children.

3

What to Talk About, Part 1

One way to begin this incremental process of discussing sex and marriage is to talk about modesty. Granted, each family will likely have its own particular view of what is modest, but all families interested in following biblical principles will be concerned about modesty. Modesty, like all other guidelines, must be rooted in biblical soil to effectively point your children to Christ. In 1 Timothy 2, modesty is tied to a lifestyle that is appropriate for those who worship God. Paul is, in effect, stating that modesty is consistent with moral purity and marriage. Thus, when you instruct your young children to dress and act with modesty, you should also connect this standard to loving God and preparing for marriage. Even with very young children you can explain that there are certain parts of the body that are special and reserved for one's husband or wife alone.

The same way of thinking also applies to physical contact and affection. Affectionate physical contact is special. While is it good and appropriate for immediate family members to show physical affection for each other, it should be stressed that even this contact must be done with modesty in mind.

Affectionate contact that includes kissing, touching and holding beyond the standards of biblical modesty set by your family is to be reserved for marriage. Aggressive, consistent teaching in these two areas— modesty and physical contact—will prepare both you and your children for the more intimate details required when discussing the particulars of sexuality. Because of the overt sexual themes of our culture, talking about specific sexual sins at increasingly younger ages is essential. Gay marriage, oral sex, hot bodies and similar expressions are now a part of daily life and conversation. Terms such as these may appear in commercials or news programs at any time during the day. Your elementary school children will hear them at school, on the playground, or even at church.

As a parent, you must make it your concern to know what your children are hearing when you are not around. This is not as difficult to do as you might think. Find a teacher who works with your child's grade level and find out what they hear being discussed. Ask older siblings or children in your church what things are being discussed by children similar in age to yours. Listen carefully to the conversations your children have with other kids. Find out what TV programs and movies your child's friends are watching and watch them yourself occasionally. Listen carefully to your children and encourage them to discuss with you the things they see and hear. By being faithful in this area you will learn what your kids are being exposed to. This will tell you what you need to address with them, and when. If your eight-year-old child is hearing about oral sex (and he very well may be) he needs to hear from you how he should process this information. If you have been careful to talk about biblical guidelines for modesty and physical contact, you will already have a context for this discussion. You can then say that oral sex is a form of kissing that is inappropriate outside of marriage, and it is unwise for your child to be a part of conversations where this is talked about.

This discussion also connects to the topic of friendship: What is pleasing to God in everyday life? With whom should we spend our time? To whom should we pay attention? This is a necessary application of following the directives of Deuteronomy 6:4-7. Your goal here is to have your children arrive at the point where the instruction of Proverbs 6:20-24 becomes reality for them. These two passages are two sides of the same coin. On the one side, you want to be talking to your children about God in everyday life situations. The other side of the coin is for when your children buy into your teaching so that it speaks to them when you are not with them. This process is what I mean by an incremental approach.

There does come the time though when you will begin to bring all of these things together in a more intentional (though still ongoing) conversation about sexuality. For most children, this intentional phase should occur between ages ten and twelve. Because of the ubiquitous sexual bent of our culture, it would be unwise to wait longer than this time frame if you want to have credibility with your children. The intentional discussion definitely should occur before the onset of puberty for both boys and girls. It is not a good thing for children to begin to experience biological changes in their body and not have a biblical, loving context in which to place them. This time frame means that you should prepare for a number of intentional discussions about sexuality and marriage.

These discussions would then form the foundation for future talks about sexuality and marriage with your children until they become married.

- Understanding that puberty is part of God's plan for preparing for marriage.

- The physical changes that occur with puberty.

- How these changes are preparing the body for sexual activity in marriage.

- Modest, discreet descriptions of what happens in sexual intercourse.

- The role of sexual intercourse in:
  - Intimacy and pleasure
  - Procreation
  - Expression of unity in the one-flesh relationship
  - Worship of God

- How loving and fearing God impacts sexual attraction

- How to begin loving the husband or wife that God will bring in the future.

4

What to Talk About, Part 2

As previously mentioned, these intentional discussions would be the basis for ongoing conversations about marriage and sexuality throughout the teenage years and beyond. The talk that the father in Proverbs 7 has with his son is an example of the incremental approach. He took advantage of a situation when it presented itself. The more formal, intentional discussions have their basis in passages like Genesis 1-2, Psalm 139, Song of Solomon, and Ephesians 5:25-33.

Here are some of the topics you should discuss in these intentional discussions:

- Puberty is part of God's plan for preparing for marriage.
- Anatomical changes that occur with puberty.
- These changes are preparing the body for sexual activity in marriage.
- Modest, discreet descriptions of what happens in sexual intercourse.
- The role of sexual intercourse in:
  - Intimacy and pleasure
  - Procreation

- Expression of unity in the one-flesh relationship
- Worship of God
- Loving and fearing God impacts sexual attraction.
- How to begin loving the husband or wife that God will bring in the future.

Each of these topics deserves thoughtful preparation and planning. While each of these points share common themes that apply to everyone, it is important to make these discussions personal – tailored to the unique life experience of each child. A dispassionate, academic discussion is not helpful in this context. Sexuality is deeply personal, and it must be understood from God's perspective. But while sexuality is personal in nature, it is not designed to be self-centered. Rather, all of the topics listed above are best understood by remembering that sex is to take place in the context of serving someone else, your marriage partner. (1 John 3:16 & 4:7-12) Sex is not primarily for personal enjoyment. Sex is primarily for bringing glory to God in the context of a one-flesh relationship between husband and wife. Even then, sex is not only for the husband and wife, because all the components of sexual activity have the capacity to bring another person, a baby, into the world.

The Specifics

While I will not go into graphic detail on each of the points mentioned above, I will make at least one explicit example. You can use the reasoning contained in this example as a guide for addressing the remaining issues. Puberty involves anatomical changes that prepare your children for sexual intercourse and having children. Now, as already stated, there is more to sexual intimacy than just having children. That is certainly true, but let's also not miss the obvious. The physical changes that come with puberty are about the ability to have children. From God's perspective and mandate, this refers to sexual intercourse in marriage.

By separating sexual intimacy from marriage our culture has made this issue more challenging in at least two ways. The first way is the overt sexual focus that we have mentioned. Our society is determined to remove marriage as a requirement for sexual activity and to redefine the concept of family. Puberty is then seen as a rite of passage into adulthood without considering marriage at all. Thus, the physiological changes that do occur are not seen as preparation for marriage but as preparation for being an adult. This defies the creation mandate for which man was created.

The second way is more subtle but just as challenging. The age for getting married is moving increasingly farther away from the age of puberty. In most cultures in the world today, and up until recent history in Western culture, it was not uncommon for couples to marry within a few years of puberty. Now, a more likely time span is ten to fifteen years. This underscores the importance of helping your children see that sexual activity is not self-serving, but must be first and foremost pleasing to God. First Corinthians 6:18-20 makes this point with clarity. Our bodies are not our own to use for our own sexual pleasures. Sexual activity is to glorify God. Your children must understand what is happening to their bodies and why, but they must also understand that there will likely be a prolonged period before they may engage in the activities that these changes make possible. You must stress that these changes are happening so that they can bring glory and honor to God. This must not be an extra thought tagged on at the end of the discussion. The physical changes are brought about by God for his honor. Your child's body is not his own to do with as he pleases.

For example, as a result of what occurs at puberty there is now the possibility for sexual attraction and related thoughts to occur. These types of thoughts are to be associated with one's marriage partner (Proverbs 5:15-21). Therefore, before marriage it is not okay to engage in thoughts and activities that prepare the body for sexual intercourse. Erections in men and vaginal lubrication in women will be part of your discussions with your children. It is important to note that not every occurrence of an erection or lubrication is inappropriate. These occurrences are not voluntary, but part of the physical maturation process. What must be avoided is indulging in sexual thoughts and lust towards another person or for self-pleasure. For more on this, see the chapter on self-pleasure.

As Christians we must do better than this for our young people. Proverbs 6:20-24 teaches that your words of instruction to your children will help protect them from sexual immorality and its allure. This is what Proverbs 6:22 says:

> *When you walk, they will guide you;*
> *when you sleep, they will watch over you;*
> *when you awake, they will speak to you.*

"They" in this verse refers to the words of parental instruction. This means instructing your children how to think about the physical changes taking place in their bodies, so that they will please God and not fall into the trap of sexual sin. You want to help your children see the danger of sexual arousal outside of marriage. If their mind-set is to live intentionally for the glory and honor of God and if they understand that their bodies are not their own but the temple of the Holy Spirit, the opportunity exists to gain victory when unchecked sexual arousal could otherwise be a dominating pattern that leads to sexual temptation, lust and other sexual sins. This is what verse 24 of chapter 6 offers as an encouragement and a defense when children love God's commands from the heart. These commands will result in:

> *keeping you from the immoral woman,*
> *from the smooth tongue of the wayward wife.*

There are a number of appropriate ways to talk about the physical aspects of sexuality and puberty–but they must all be tied to marriage and living for the glory of God. Your child needs to know why his or her body reacts the way that it does in particular situations. But more importantly, your children need to realize that their hearts must be turned to Christ and his ways. Allowing their minds to entertain sexual scenarios about others violates God's intended purpose for sex in marriage. Loving God from the heart is the only protection from these attacks of the world and the flesh. Only the wonder of knowing and living for God's glory can overcome the powerful temptations of sexual sin. Again, that is why the incremental approach is important. You can't just introduce the idea of living for the glory of God when it is time to talk about sexual things. That needs to be a lifelong pursuit. The next chapter will have more to say about this.

It is possible that you, parent, may not have this view of sexuality yourself. It is also possible that you may have some unresolved guilt about your own sexual history, or even the current state of your thought life. That is when you must cry out to Christ and experience his forgiveness. He paid the penalty for your sins on the cross and even now intercedes for you. You can know God's complete forgiveness and healing from your own sins. That forgiveness will enable you to lead your children to honor God in their understanding of sexuality.

Honoring God

So, as you talk to your children, the aspect of other-centeredness is essential (1 John 4:7-12). Self-gratification and God-pleasing sexual activity are polar opposites. Yes, it is true that biblically-based sex does have the capacity to bring great pleasure, but having this pleasure must not be the primary goal of sexual activity. This is the light in which you must discuss the changes coming to your child's body. I pray that you will be able to discuss all the facets of sexuality in light of God's wonderful provision of marriage and the privilege of living for his glory and honor. This is only possible as you and your children grasp the depth of what Jesus Christ accomplished on the cross.

Next we will look at a positive way to honor God in the face of the temptation that your children will face.

5

What about Sexual Attraction?

Any conversation with your children about sex and marriage would be incomplete without discussing sexual attraction. This topic often lacks biblical clarity for Christians because it is most commonly discussed outside its biblical context. The Bible is clear: sex is reserved for marriage. If one is attracted to sexual activity, that attraction can be pleasing to God only when it is focused on its expression within marriage.

On the other hand, I am not saying that we should not appreciate—and even, in a proper sense, be attracted by beauty. But the Bible makes a distinction between admiration of beauty and sexual attraction. The beauty of Job's daughters was recognized throughout the land. That is not the same as saying that people throughout the land desired them sexually. On the other hand, Proverbs 5:19 speaks of being captivated (NIV) or intoxicated (ESV) by love for one's wife. The public admiration of physical beauty is appropriate when there is no intimacy or lust involved. Sexual attraction, though, is to be restricted and private.

Unlike the appreciation of physical beauty,

biblical sexual attraction leads to intimate knowledge of the person being admired.

Biblical sexual attraction must involve at least these four qualities:

- Worship of God
- Intimacy and pleasure
- The purpose of procreation
- Expression of unity in the one-flesh relationship

In his book, The God of Sex, Dr. Peter Jones gives a thorough and compelling biblical argument for this view of sexual attraction. Biblical sexual attraction goes far beyond what the world calls sexual attraction, and marriage is absolutely essential if God is going to be honored when you or your children think about sex.

In this culture, we have the myth of the red-blooded American male. The idea is that when male or female hormones are at work, sexual attraction can't be helped; it is involuntary. That may be the world's understanding, but it is rooted in the humanistic, Darwinian thought that sex is primarily a biological function and that sexual attraction is necessary to ensure that humans keep breeding. Both your sons and daughters must be taught that such thinking is unbiblical and displeasing to God. Sex and marriage are not the products of a long evolutionary process. Rather, they are part of God's mandate for man at creation to glorify God as he occupied and controlled the earth.

Christ warns against lust leading to adultery of the heart. Paul insists that Christians are not to live life as the world does, becoming dominated by sensuality. Sensuality is what passes for sexual attraction in this culture–but sensuality is actually the opposite of biblical sexual attraction.

That is why it is vital that sexual activity be rooted in the context of marriage. Sexual attraction is to be private and deeply personal between husband and wife. Biblical sexual attraction is not primarily physical attraction. Look with at me at Proverbs 5:15-21, and you will see why this is true.

> [15] *Drink water from your own cistern,*
> *running water from your own well.*
> [16] *Should your springs overflow in the streets,*
> *your streams of water in the public squares?*
> [17] *Let them be yours alone,*
> *never to be shared with strangers.*
> [18] *May your fountain be blessed,*
> *and may you rejoice in the wife of your youth.*
> [19] *A loving doe, a graceful deer –*
> *may her breasts satisfy you always,*
> *may you ever be captivated by her love.*
> [20] *Why be captivated, my son, by an adulteress?*
> *Why embrace the bosom of another man's wife?*
> [21] *For a man's ways are in full view of the* LORD,
> *and he examines all his paths.*

Note the personal nature of this instruction. The husband's thoughts are not to be public, but private. He is not to look at other women the way he looks at his wife. There is no doubt that the husband is to be sexually attracted to his wife and her body. But note carefully that this attraction is not physical at the core. The passage does not say if one's wife meets certain culturally accepted criteria then he is to be attracted to her. Not at all. Rather, this view of sexual attraction is intensely biblical and personal. Since every woman's body is different–in some cases dramatically different–from other women's bodies, it cannot be the size and shape of her body that is the basis of a husband being captivated and intoxicated by her. The four relational components listed at the beginning of this chapter form the basis of the husband's intoxication for his wife. That is how appreciation of physical beauty and biblical sexual attraction differentiate themselves. Physical beauty can be admired by many. But sexual attraction is only for one's marriage partner.

Sexual attraction outside of marriage will lead to lust and, eventually, torment. It is important to teach this truth to both your daughters and your sons. In Galatians 5:19-21, sensuality is listed as one of the deeds of the flesh. The Spirit's fruit of self-control is what counters sensuality. The Holy Spirit's fruit of self-control is not the anguished self-denial of living with unmet desires. Biblical self-control is rooted in the fact that God has better things prepared for his people in sexual relations than we can possibly imagine. That is the view of self-control that God wants you to teach your children. That is the view they will need in order to withstand the sexual onslaught of modern culture. What the world offers as sexual attractiveness is a lie. It never satisfies. It only produces an uncontrollable hunger for more and more sex. Sexual attraction in this context is simply lust, and it is destructive to all it controls.

As we mentioned earlier, true biblical sexual attraction can only be found in the context of marriage. This attraction will feature a love and worship of God, and an intimacy and pleasure that can only come when two people are more committed to God than they are to each other. The world knows nothing of this self-sacrificing intimacy. Don't let your children be sold a counterfeit view of sexual attraction that involves only physical stimulation and titillation. God has something far better for them. God is the God of Sex. Call your children to entrust themselves to him as they think about sex and marriage.

6

Love Your Spouse Before You Know Them

When helping your children address the tempt-ation of sexual arousal before marriage, the first consideration is encouraging your children to focus on bringing honor to God instead of follow-ing the path of self-pleasure. This encouragement needs to be practical and not just theoretical; the opportunities for temptation to sexual arousal are everywhere in our culture. Being "turned on" is seen as a natural response in our culture (a response to be exploited by advertisers and cheerleaders alike.) Flirtation is portrayed as harmless. Teenagers must avoid these traps and begin loving the person they will someday marry—right now! But how? Parents and church leaders must teach our teens, by precept and example, not to yield to temptations to think sexual thoughts about someone to whom they are not married.

The Bible does not condone a "try before you buy" policy with regard to sexual relations. According to Matthew 5:28, lust in the heart is as wrong as sexual sin in the flesh; sex is part of the marriage covenant and has no place outside of marriage, mentally or physically. Even if your children remain single through adulthood, that relationship status does not change the reality that sexual relationships are to take place only in the context of marriage. Sexual activity, including the feelings of sexual arousal for another person to whom you are not married, does not honor God. It is the sin of lust.

Sexual arousal, therefore, is not a random, biological reaction as our culture teaches. Sexual arousal is always deeply personal. It can be really good or really devastating, but it is always personal. When this arousal occurs outside of marriage it is a personal offense to God and his directive that sex is designed for marriage. Sexual longings outside of marriage rail against the path that God has called you and your teenagers to follow. Sexual arousal towards someone you are not married to is a willful, sensual use of another person for your own selfish indulgence. It is an attempt to gain pleasure from someone else without their knowledge. This kind of lust is a form of mental stalking, wherein someone else's body is used to gain pleasure. This practice only reinforces the notion that sex is innately selfish and an entitlement.

Make no mistake. Sexual arousal outside of marriage is natural—just as greed, anger, lying, and jealousy are also natural; being natural, however, is not always a good thing. We are born with natural desires that condemn us to hell apart from the saving work of Christ. No one has any trouble saying that giving into the natural desire of anger as a justification for violence is a bad thing. Yet, when it comes to sexual arousal, it is somehow okay for our natural desires to dominate. Natural anger left unchecked will result in bullying, violence and even death. Natural sexual arousal left unchecked results in even more devastating consequences than anger does. It is time for Christian parents and leaders to step up and encourage our children to honor God when faced with sexual arousal. We must teach them that only honoring and loving God will help them reserve these desires for marriage.

At this point, learning to show love to the person you will marry comes in to play. Instead of yielding to temptations to look at someone sexually before you are married, ask God to help you honor your future spouse with your eyes and with your mind. You don't even have to know your spouse yet to begin to honor and love them. Galatians 5:16-6:10 teaches us that we constantly face two opposing desires: desires given by God's Spirit and desires that come from our flesh. Paul tells us that what we plant today will be found growing later. Don't let the crop that grows in your children's lives be impurity and sexual immorality. Teach them, from Galatians and elsewhere, what godly desires look like, and teach them to submit to those desires daily. Then, and only then, will your children see the harvest of faithfulness and self-control grow in their lives. In this way, even if you remain single you can avoid sensual indulgence at someone else's expense.

It is important here to distinguish between the admiration of beauty and sexual lust. There are people who are physically beautiful, even stunningly beautiful. It is a good thing to appreciate physical beauty. It is a bad thing to be the equivalent of a sexual stalker and imagine sexual activity with another person to whom you are not married. For example, a husband should desire his wife sexually

(Proverbs 5:15-20). He may also admire the beauty of other women. But what he must not do is imagine what it would be like to have sexual engagement, in any form, with someone other than his wife. This same principle would apply to any man or woman who is not married.

The above approach represents a significant departure from the way our culture views sexual attraction: we are not helpless victims of sexually stimulated hormones. As also noted above, we humans experience other strong physical reactions produced by anger or greed or bitterness. Even the non-Christian world would argue that such reactions must be controlled and redirected. But sexual arousal—that is a different story. There is sensual pleasure to be had—and there is money to be made in advertising, fashion, and pornography.

The thought process we have been talking about provides a positive alternative to our culture's fatal attraction to sexual arousal. Remember the warning of the father in Proverbs 7: entertaining sexual arousal leads to the bedrooms of death. Our children need to know that marriage and sex are a unique and crucial combination in God's design for occupying and controlling the earth for his glory. When marriage and sex are separated we simply cannot function as God intended. If you want your children to honor God with their lives, teach them how to begin loving the person they will one day marry. Help them to see the dangers of sexual arousal outside of marriage. God's ways are better than anything a sinful world has to offer.

Avoidance of sexual arousal is a special gift that, some day, your teenagers can offer to the person they marry. No, the gift will not be as humanly perfect as it could be. This area is no different than any other area of sin that we struggle with. Forgiveness and repentance, however, can make whole what once was rotten. Beauty can come from the ashes of sin. Your children need not be stained with the curse of the scarlet letter if there is genuine repentance.

Parents, you must enter the battle to teach your children what it means to view marriage and sexual relations as the Lord intended. Remember to fit this chapter in with the rest of the teaching in this book. We do have a superior way to teach our children about what our sex-crazed culture is selling. Praise God for his wonderful provision of marriage and sex. Let us not separate them any longer.

7

Celebrate Sexual Purity

The final point that needs to be covered concerning talking to your children about sex and marriage is the joyous pursuit of sexual purity. Sexual purity is the eager and aggressive commitment to trusting God's parameters for sexual conduct. This should be a pursuit of joy. Sexual purity must not be defined only as a negative. The pursuit of sexual purity is not only to avoid what is wrong but to eagerly pursue what is right. In this case, what is right is a passionate commitment to engage in sexual matters as God has instructed in his Word. Such purity leads to an active worship of God in all of life. That is something that you can talk about without hesitation with your children. Trusting God with their sexuality is the absolute best thing that anyone can do. You do not have to discuss every area of sexual perversion in order to prepare children for combating sexual sin. To be sure, you should be prepared to discuss questions about the sexual sin that is rampant in our culture, but even this must be in the context that God's ways are superior to the natural practice of this world.

Preparing your children to combat sexual sin can and should begin very early. It is never too soon to say that marriage is a wonderful blessing from God. When any discussions of sexuality arise, you should always point out what is appropriate for marriage and what is not. Over time your explanations will need to be more specific, until finally you arrive at the franker discussions needed to address the onset of puberty. But in the context of ongoing conversations, extending over years, you have the privilege of positioning sexual behavior positively, within marriage. Then, you have natural opportunities to demonstrate that when people choose to disobey God's directives for sexuality, bad things happen.

Parents, you must not shy away from this point. Spiritual warfare is raging around you and your children at this point. Sexual purity is depicted in our culture as a joyless life of self-denial and struggle. But that is not what God teaches about sexual purity. Sexual purity in marriage is a cause for celebration. It is too easy to think that sexual purity means no sexual activity or dull boring activity. At least, that is what the enemy of your soul wants you and your children to think. In contrast, Hebrews 13:4 says the marriage bed must be kept pure and undefiled. Sex that is pure is sex that brings honor to God and joy to his people. It takes place in marriage.

A brief history is helpful here. The 1960s are described as the era of sexual revolution. Once again, as so often over the course of human history, man decided it was stupid to follow God's plan for sexuality. Free love and free sex were the battle cry of that time. People began to believe the lies that sex was the rite of passage to personal liberation.

Well, what has happened since that time? Households with married mothers and fathers are no longer the norm, either statistically or ideologically in Western culture. Sexually transmitted diseases are rampant. Pornography is destroying men and their families at an alarming rate. Lust knows no boundaries and enslaves people from all walks of life. Treatment for depression is now a multi-billion dollar industry. Divorce is common. Marriage is no longer essential for raising children. It would be naïve to think that the pursuit of godless sex outside of marriage is unrelated to all of the above. Rather, these behaviors happen when sexual purity in marriage is exchanged for the lies of the world.

This theme is the way to begin and end discussions with your children about marriage and sex. God's ways are always better. God knows more about sexual pleasure than anyone else–he designed it for his glory. Our God is not to be mocked. Disregarding his commands regarding sexual purity and marriage will lead only to emptiness, despair and personal destruction. Romans 1:18-32 is clear on this point. But God has great things in store for those who will trust him. You must passionately believe this about sexuality and marriage in order to encourage your children to trust God in this area.

Sadly, there is also instruction that must be given about sexual perversion and lust. There are many excellent books and materials to help. I urge you to accept God's call to celebrate sexual purity within marriage. Encourage your children with this biblical perspective.

As we have seen, sexual sin creates relational wreckage and pain. Perhaps your life has been so negatively impacted by sexual sin that you are reluctant to talk with your children about obeying God in marriage and sexuality. In that case, let me encourage you with the power of the gospel. The cross of Christ can bring wholeness to your life. We all stand in need of the powerful grace of God. Seek his grace in the gospel of Jesus Christ. You can know the life-changing grace extended in God's forgiveness. Your children are not perfect either. They will most likely fall short at some point in their battle with sexual sin. They need to know that the gospel can restore purity. They can become as white as snow through the redeeming work of Christ. Make this wonderful message of the gospel a part of your discussions about marriage and sexuality. Both you and your children need to hear it. It is the only message that brings hope to the devastation of sexual sin.

8

Application: Safe Sex, an Urban Legend

Teaching your children to honor God's authority by obeying quickly and pleasantly has many blessings. One of these blessings is to learn to avoid the world's wisdom, no matter how attractive it may appear. For example, there is the lie that there can be safe sex outside of marriage.

Modern man, in his proverbial darkened state, plunges ever deeper into darkness by seeking new and creative ways to say Yes to sex outside of marriage. This thinking brings a rising tide of the health risks and emotional wreckage that comes from the practice of "safe sex."

Safe sex outside of marriage is a deadly oxymoron of modern life. The truth is that any sex outside of marriage is anything but safe! Extramarital sex is one of the most dangerous activities that people can engage in. A few moments of pleasure are stupidly traded for a life of worry, insecurity and physical danger. Within one generation, the slide into immorality has gone from, "Can I get her to kiss me on the first date?" to, "Can I..." Well, you know what follows. The words of Solomon, 3,000 years ago, still ring true:

Can a man scoop fire into his lap
without his clothes being burned?
Can a man walk on hot coals
without his feet being scorched?
So is he who sleeps with another man's wife;
no one who touches her will go unpunished.

(Proverbs 6:27-29)

As Romans says, the truth of God has been exchanged for a lie. In this case, the lie is that there is safe sex outside of marriage. For example a young couple, using certain types of contraceptives, may, in fact, prevent the spread of a certain type of disease or infection or a pregnancy. But what about the spiritual damage that is being done every time this young couple engages in "protected" sexual activity? Their very souls are laid open to be ravaged by lies, deceit and insecurity. They are being wounded with wounds that may never heal. They will learn the fleeting enticements of self-pleasure instead of the treasures of sensitivity and selfless love. Relationships that have "protected" sex are plagued with fear, doubt, and even multiple forms of abuse. Divorce rates are up, spousal and domestic abuse is rampant, and abortions are considered to be a necessary part of life. This is the grim harvest of safe sex.

The world teaches that you can have sex any way, anytime you want to. Safe, protected sex outside of marriage is a modern urban legend, a hideous lie that waits to devour your children. Christian, have the courage to tell your children the truth about what constitutes sex that is safe. The marriage bed alone is the one place where sex is truly protected and is truly safe.

9

Application: Thoughts about Self-pleasure and Masturbation

Masturbation is an awkward topic to discuss. Conventional wisdom just assumes it is a natural act that everyone does. But as we have seen, natural is not always good. Another thing that is universally agreed upon about masturbation is that it is a sexual act. This provides the opportunity to frame the discussion about masturbation in a biblical context. Remember the foundational concept we looked at in the first chapter:

> The whole of the Christian life, in fact, is focused on the sacrificial and selfless love of others done in imitation of Christ. Therefore, sex cannot be both God honoring and self serving.

By using this principle as a lens to look at sexual activity we can gain a biblical view of how to think about masturbation. Human sexuality was designed by God for marriage. Self-pleasure is not part of this picture. A key ingredient for having a biblically healthy sexual relationship in marriage is for both partners to be focused on how they can please the other and honor God. If self-pleasure becomes the goal, sex can turn from a rich blessing into a curse. So, then how does indulging in self-pleasure before marriage help prepare a person to become a sensitive, caring and unselfish marriage partner? Short answer, it doesn't.

Masturbation is about self-pleasure. Therefore, masturbation doesn't make for a better, biblical marriage. Rather masturbation focuses the attention on self, which is never a good thing. Ephesians 4:19 sharply contrasts sensitivity with sensuality. Paul warns here that losing sensitivity, or becoming callous, results in sensuality. In Galatians 5:19 sensuality is one of the deeds of the flesh that is dominated by the impact of the sinful nature with which we were born. Sensuality is like selfishness on steroids, especially with regard to sexual sin. Sensitivity, in contrast, means we are to serve others rather than ourselves.

Well, then, what about before marriage? Masturbation is clearly understood to be a sexual activity. It is also clear that God commands that marriage is the place where sexual activity is to take place. So, masturbation isn't helpful before marriage either. Where does that leave us regarding the appropriateness of masturbation? Simply put, masturbation is not a good idea for people who want to honor God.

One indicator of whether or not a behavior is honorable is if you can pray for God's blessing and help to do the particular behavior. For example, there is no problem with asking God to help you to remain pure in thought and deed before marriage. It is a good thing for a husband to ask God for strength to be more sensitive to his wife and to honor her. But would these same type of prayers work for asking God to bless masturbation for his glory?

Many will, no doubt, object to this conclusion because it doesn't fit with accepted view of our culture and even with that of many Christians. After all, masturbation is an accepted practice according to health care providers, psychologists, and respected educators. But this same argument could be used to support sex outside of marriage.

As far as public opinion goes, in a 2008 Pew Research poll only 35 percent thought that sex between unmarried adults was morally wrong. Twenty two percent thought this behavior morally right, while 37 percent believed that sex between unmarried adults was not a moral issue. Not much help in the court of public opinion.

Biblically speaking, I believe we are left with the conclusion that masturbation is not a good idea. This practice falls outside the guidelines of loving God and loving others as the top priority for a Christian. There is certainly no command to masturbate. At the very least it is a selfish act. In this broad sense masturbation is best categorized as sinful activity. It falls into the category of sensuality rather than sensitivity.

Having established this, can we now say "problem solved," as in, tell your children not to masturbate and if they are masturbating, simply tell them to stop?

Hardly.

The real damage done by masturbation is the aftermath of doubt, loneliness, guilt, and enslavement. This is probably the most important biblical objection to masturbation. Parent, this is where you must be sensitive in talking about masturbation with your teenagers. We said earlier that talking about masturbation is awkward. It is awkward because it is not something that is good. It is embarrassing. The vast majority, if not all, of masturbation is driven by lust. Let's look at Ephesians 4:19 again:

"Having lost all sensitivity, they have given themselves over to sensuality so as to indulge in every kind of impurity, with a continual lust for more."

This painfully describes the legacy of masturbation. Sensitivity is required to help you help your children. Masturbation does not draw your children closer to God. It is an attempt to solve a problem in one's own strength. The problem is sexual arousal or attraction. The solution of the flesh is masturbation. The answer of the Spirit is trust in God's provision. You and your children are not the victims of biological urges.

Let's briefly work through the aftermath of masturbation.

Doubt

Because masturbation cannot be pursued with confidence that it is God's blessing to answer one's deep struggles, true dependence upon God cannot be the result. Doubt is the result. As James says, one who doubts is "like a wave of the sea, blown and tossed about by the wind." Doubt does not bring peace, but turmoil. Your teenager may have deeper issues than just not getting his homework done. He or she may be struggling with doubt regarding masturbation.

Loneliness

Masturbation is a lonely activity. It is not something that is shared with others. It can lead to insecurity, inordinate self-centeredness or narcissism. Because masturbation is so self-consuming it is a functional roadblock to marital intimacy. Little thought is given to a potential marriage partner, just the pursuit of self-pleasure. In this sense, the loneliness of masturbation is the opposite of the one-flesh union of marriage, where the husband and wife complete each other. Even before sin entered the world, God said it was not good for man to be alone. Masturbation and the pursuit of self-pleasure says being alone is just fine. Masturbation teaches that self-satisfaction must come first before the satisfaction of a wife. This thinking is highly destructive to any marriage relationship. So doubt is followed by loneliness. What follows next is guilt.

Guilt

Guilt is the next thing to consider. If there is no confidence that a good thing is being done, guilt is not far behind. In addition to doubt, your teenager is now plagued by guilt. Doubts morph into guilt and defensiveness. Deep inside, your teenagers know that continued masturbation is not healthy and they think it really isn't something they can ask about or get help with. Often, teenagers will pray that they can stop, but they are unsure of what to pray for. Repeated attempts to stop only lead to discouragement and then more doubt about why God doesn't help them stop. Your teenager is caught in a vicious cycle of lust that craves for more and more appeasement of the desires of the flesh. This leads to a crippling guilt and to enslavement. It is a great blessing for your teenagers to trust Christ for forgiveness for any sin, including lust and masturbation. Do not be shy in encouraging them to know that Christ does forgive and heal the wounds caused by the pursuit of self-pleasure.

Enslavement

For some teenagers, what was once occasional and sporadic can become a dominate pattern. No matter how frequently masturbation occurs, it is never enough, just as Paul said. At this point, pornography and lustful thoughts may also fuel the fires of anticipation. Enslavement is now total.

Or is it? Our gracious God does have a way out from darkness into the light. It's important that your children start facing this awful sin by understanding the freeing truth about God's grace, given to us through his Son. Self-pleasure is a denial of God's plan and generous provision for our lives. Our Savior though has a different plan. God does not keep a record of sins, even masturbation. Look at Psalm 130:1-4:

> *From the depths of despair, O Lord,*
> *I call for your help.*
> *Hear my cry, O Lord.*
> *Pay attention to my prayer.*
> *Lord, if you kept a record of our sins,*
> *who, O Lord, could ever survive?*
> *But you offer forgiveness,*
> *that we might learn to fear you.*

Here is what Jesus says to your teenager, "I am the light of the world. Whoever follows me will never walk in darkness, but will have the light of life." There is a way out of the darkness of sin!

Parent, your child must understand the order of how this happens. They cannot blot out or clean up their "darkness," and then learn to become like Christ. These are the steps:

- First, they are forgiven.

- Second, they follow Jesus,

- Third, they walk in the light of life.

They, like everyone else, cannot pursue a life of Christlikeness by ceasing self-service and masturbation. Self-service and masturbation will cease as they seek to think, act, and in every way imitate the life of Christ. It is vital your approach to your children not be one of condemnation or judgment, but one of compassion.

Trusting in God's provision for sex and marriage

Obviously, the acts of masturbation must stop. But more importantly, the tragically self-reliant unbiblical thinking that helped encourage masturbation must also stop. Without repentance and new thoughts about God's provision of sex in marriage your teenager will only be tormented with the overwhelming temptation to fall back into relying again on masturbation and out-of-control lust to solve his problems. As we have seen, lust is a cruel master. Help your child to see it is not the Holy Spirit who is urging masturbation as the solution to their longings.

This is where the principles we looked at earlier can make a huge difference. Sex is not for self-pleasure. God is not one to dangle a carrot of hope for the far distant future. God promises a rich relationship now for those who trust him and want to know him. Do what is necessary to help your teenager see the ugliness of the lie of masturbation. You can't force this view on them. Rather, you have to make it attractive to yourself, before you can offer this truth to others. Parent, your view of sex and marriage must also be aligned with Scripture if you are to help your children to trust God.

Take the time to have the relationship with your children to allow you to talk about the awkward things. Work through the things we have discussed in the earlier chapters. Love them and delight in them for who they are, not for who you want them to be. It is easy to have a conversation about the latest cell phone you want to give them. But having conversations about trusting God and Christ's redemptive power with their thoughts of sex and marriage—it doesn't get any better.

PART 2

10

A First Conversation

Conversation between Dad and Son (about 11)

"Sean, while the other kids and Mom are out shopping, there is something I want to talk to you about."

"Uh, do I have a choice?"

"No, not really, but this is something that I need to do to be a good dad to you."

"Dad, is this really necessary?"

"Yep. I noticed at the soccer game that some of the guys were talking pretty explicitly about certain girls."

"Yeah, Dad. They do that all the time."

"Well, I know that you are only eleven, but I also know that one day you will probably get married."

"Daaad."

"I know, it is kind of awkward for me too. You remember when we read about the father talking to his son about the immoral woman in Proverbs 7 and he was warning him not to be deceived like the young idiot in the story?"

"Yeah."

"Well, that is why I have to have these talks with you. Your mom and I have been talking to you for a long time about how special marriage is. "

"I know Dad!"

"Okay. Well, what I realized is that it is time to begin being more specific. You will be hearing other kids talking more and more about sex, but not about sex and marriage. Over the next few years we will need to have several talks about helping you to understand how dangerous it is to talk about sexual things apart from marriage. Kids often think it is cool, but it really is damaging. Just like the young man in Proverbs 7, thinking about sex without being married will lead to life being a painful mess. Anyway, I just wanted you to know that we will be talking about this. Thanks for listening today. I love you."

"Dad, do we really have to do this? It is really weird."

"I know, but, yes we do. Remember it is kind of hard for me as well. Hang in there, we will get through it."

11

Conversation about Women

Conversation between Dad and 14-year-old Son

This conversation illustrates what you should be praying for as your talks progress over time. This conversation is one that is typical after you get started.

"Hey Sean, there is something I want to talk with you about."

"Dad, is this one of your talks about sex and marriage?'

"How did you know?"

"Well that last commercial was pretty obvious. I was like, 'no way Dad's going to let that go.' I was thinking about trying to go back to my room, but I figured you would just track me down anyway."

"Very perceptive."

"Not really. You're literally that predictable. But it's not that bad I guess. When you started with all this, I wasn't real excited about it. But now, I mean, it could be worse. But it is still a little weird."

"I know, it is for me too. I appreciate you hanging in there with me. You are right, that commercial illustrates how our culture messes things up. I mean what does a woman with a revealing top have to do with selling chips?"

"Well, I know what my friends would say. They are both hot."

"Uh, right. This is exactly what I have been trying to talk to you about. "Hot" in this case means that the woman is somehow sexually desirable because of the particular shape of her body. But let's follow up. Presenting the girl in the commercial that way gives a false expectation of sexual pleasure. The commercial is attempting to say that if a female looks like the girl with the chips that she will be a pleasing sexual partner."

"Yeah, Dad, I get that part."

"Okay, but suppose you married someone who didn't look like the girl with chips, does that mean she would not be desirable as a wife? You see, this commercial is really unkind to women. It says they have to look a certain way to please men. And if a woman does not look like that, she is not really desirable, or as you friends put it, "hot."

"Yeah, I remember, God says a gentle heart or whatever is true beauty. But I hope my wife still looks good."

"Yep. The implication is that if a woman doesn't look like that she won't be a good wife. The Bible teaches us that that is not true. Actually it is a lie that hurts marriages. That kind of cultural standard of being "hot" is one of the reasons we have a high divorce rate."

"Dad, I am fourteen. I'm not exactly getting married next week."

"I know, but, it is really important to keep sexual thoughts for your wife and not the chip girl."

"I get it, Dad. But it's hard because everybody keeps talking about it at school."

"Sadly, it is no different for most of the men I know, too. Thanks for talking about this. I really appreciate it! Your mom and I will keep praying for you."

"Yeah, thanks Dad. We done now?"

12

Conversation about Sex and Babies

Conversation between Mom and 16-year-old Daughter

This is a conversation to have with your older teenagers. This one happens as a result of regularly engaging your kids about maintaining a biblical worldview of sex and marriage. The discussion is between a mom and her sixteen-year-old daughter. The conversation shows how the mom has worked to be able to have good, productive communication with her daughter.

"Hey Mom, so, I have a question for you about, um … about the sex stuff and marriage you've been talking about."

"Great, let's hear it."

"Okay, just please don't get too upset. It is about something from my modern history and culture class at school, you know the one with the teacher that is bashing Christians all the time."

"Thanks for the heads up! I promise, I'll be calm. You know me."

"That is exactly why I said to not get upset. Okay, here goes. My teacher said that the "true believer" Christians, the ones that are ignorant enough to think the Bible is true, think that the only reason to have sex is to have babies. Then she read a bunch of quotes that seemed to totally support her point. And some of the quotes were from people that you and Dad agree with. I know that you don't think that way, but where is she getting all this stuff? She was trying to make me feel like a complete idiot."

"Wow, thanks for bringing that up. See I'm very calm."

"For now."

"Very funny. Okay, your teacher is partly right. There are some Christians who think that way, but, like we have talked about, because of the internet search engines it is also easy to pull sound bites out of context to make a person seem to say something that they don't believe."

"I know, I know. But I still feel like I don't completely get this, you know?"

"That's okay! God designed sexual activity to accomplish many things. Having children is just one of the reasons for sexual intimacy. It is an important one, but not the only one."

"That's where I am having trouble. From what you've said, everything that happens in, you know, sex, is to make babies possible."

"That is not exactly what I said. My goal was to say that what happens in sexual relations between husband and wife makes it possible for the wife to become pregnant.

"That would really set my teacher off, implying that sex is only for married people."

"... I'm just going to stay on point here, so I don't get upset."

"Wow, score one for Mom!"

"Cute. Okay. What you have to remember is that having sex does not always result in a pregnancy. When older couples have sex the same things happen to their bodies, even though the wife can't get pregnant anymore."

"Eww, Mom! Can we skip the older people part!?!"

"Okay, okay. But I mentioned that because it demonstrates that sex is about more than having children. It is also true that some married couples are not able to have children, but they still have sex."

"But doesn't that help my teacher's argument?"

"No, not really. Remember we talked about when God created Adam and Eve, part of what he told them was to multiply and fill the earth with people?"

"Yeah."

"Well that command is something that reminds us that sex is not designed by people but by God. So, we never want to separate God's command to have sex in marriage from the reason why we have sex in the first place. In other words, all the things that go into a married couple's enjoyment of sex: sharing intimacy, caring for your spouse, having children, honoring God, all of those things are a part of the special relationship of marriage. It is actually pretty cool to see that having sex is more than what I can get out of it. From your teacher's perspective the one valid reason to have sex is to have pleasure."

"Yeah, pretty much."

"Right. Well, by understanding that God is the one who designed sex in the first place, it only makes sense that sex is best enjoyed by having it the way that he wants. So having sex outside of marriage is really very selfish."

"Well, not always, right? I mean, I know it's wrong, but some people really love each other, and they could be unselfish when they, you know, sleep together."

"Well, honey, not actually. The Bible says love is sacrificing and doing what's best for the other person. If we really love someone, we'll do what's best for them. To do that, we need to have the right perspective on who made sex and why. When we do that, we recognize God's wonderful provision for marriage means a lot more than just selfish fun. This is one reason people like your teacher say it is okay and good to have sex anytime you want. She thinks having sex is for her benefit. God is not even part of her thinking. This is one of the reasons we have so many marriage problems today. People think it is only about them and their pleasure. Does this help?"

"I think so. You certainly are more positive about sex than my teacher. All she seems to do is get mad at people that don't think like she does. Anyway, thanks for not getting too upset."

"Hey, no problem. Thanks for asking!"

13

Conversation about Self-Control

Conversation between Dad and 14-year-old son

This is an example of one of the many conversations that should happen as your children move through their teenage years.

"Hey Eric, today I want to talk with you about part of sex and marriage we have not touched on yet."

"I thought you'd talked about everything imaginable."

"Well, I guess I have talked about the physical things involved."

"Okay, awesome. So what's left?"

"Evolution."

"Dad, you don't have to go there. I get it. No apes in the family tree. Except Uncle Herb."

"Don't let your mother hear you saying that."

"Deal."

"But seriously, Eric. There are many Christians who reject evolution in theory but still live as if it were true."

"How's that?"

"Well, when it comes to love and sexual attraction, people act like it's just a natural biological drive, and not something God gives us. You remember that show on the Discovery Channel that compared human relationships with those of other species?"

"Oh yeah, the one where the guy was talking about how humans were just like every other animal, that our mating rituals or whatever just evolved. Then it showed all those clips of animals doing stuff.

"Look, when guys think they just can't help themselves from getting turned on by a girl, they are thinking like somebody who believes in evolution. See, if we're just animals like Mr. Discovery Channel says, there's no need or place for purity, it is all just an automatic biological reaction."

"Yeah, but it is just kind of, you know, automatic, right? He probably just means, like, why fight it? "

"Because purity is a gift and a command from God. It didn't evolve. Sexual relations in marriage is not something that evolved over time. It was that way from the beginning. God specifically designed sex to happen in marriage. It is not random social or evolutionary development. Does that help?"

"Sorta. Is this like what you've been saying about sex only working in marriage?'

"That's it. God made people differently than every other creature. He made us in his image. That is not true of any other creature on earth. So sex is different for people than it is for every other species. We don't have to be controlled by biological urges. God wants us to choose to have sex when he says it is best and that would be in marriage. When I was growing up I heard guys talking all the time about how they couldn't control themselves, it was just the way they were made."

"I've heard that too, I guess … are there ways? I mean, you're saying there are ways to like, control it, right?"

"I used to think there weren't, before I knew what the Bible taught. As it turns out, there are a lot of practices and habits I didn't even think were related that actually make it much easier to control your thoughts and actions."

"Okay ..."

"Things don't get any easier once you're married. If guys, or girls for that matter, think they can't control themselves before marriage then their thinking probably won't change after they get married. In other words, they still think they can't help being physically attracted to women. How do you think that works out in a marriage?"

"Let me guess. Not so good?"

"You got it. One of the reasons divorce rates are so high is because people think they can't or shouldn't control their sexual thoughts. God has something better for us. We're not controlled by biological, sexual evolution. Okay?"

"Okay ... but, how do you control it? You said the Bible says how?"

"It does. You want to talk about it soon?"

"Yeah! I mean, sure."

"All right, Eric, I'm looking forward to it."

14

Conversation about Periods

Conversation between Mom and Daughter

Mom has just explained to her daughter, Laura, that she should begin having her monthly periods soon. Laura responds this way:

"Okay, Mom, can you explain again why God would make me have periods?"

"Sure, Laura, what part didn't make sense?"

"All of it! So I have to bleed, have pain, wear pads, and be moody. Every month! I don't want to have periods."

"Sweetheart, that's not all I said. Having periods can be really hard, but not always. Even so, it is a good thing too."

"Yeah, well, it doesn't sound like it. I don't understand how hurting and bleeding happens because 'God loves me' and because he 'made me special.'"

"I know getting your period doesn't sound fun, I get that. But Laura, God made us this way. Part of trusting God is trusting that he knows what's best for us."

"I do, Mom. But I've heard girls at school talking about it, and it doesn't sound good. Some of them say it really hurts."

"Do all of them say that?"

"No. Not everyone, but a lot do. And some of the older girls call it the curse. From what you said I can see why."

"Okay, I heard that too when I was your age. It is important to remember God made women this way. It's anything but a curse. Having periods is a necessary part of having children."

"That doesn't make sense! I thought you said you get a period when you don't get pregnant."

"Honey, don't be disrespectful. Just because you're upset isn't a good reason to raise your voice."

"I'm sorry, Mom."

"I forgive you. Now, let me explain why you have to have a period. A woman's body produces an egg about once a month. If you don't become pregnant, the egg needs to be removed from your body to get ready for the next egg. Removing the egg from your body is why you have a period. It takes a lot of hard work from your body to have a baby. Everything has to be just right, which is why your body starts all over each month. That's why it gets a little messy. It's just the way God designed us. The problem is, because sin entered the world, it became very painful. Everything in life is harder because of sin. But it's still an important part of having children."

"But what if I don't want to have children, Mom?"

"Not everyone's life includes marriage and children, but it does for most of us because God designed us this way. Loving a child and putting them before yourself is one of the most God-honoring things we can do. Remember when we talked about what Paul said in Philippians about considering other people as more important than yourself?"

"Yeah, I remember. Mom, are your periods hard for you?"

"Sometimes. I don't have really bad ones like some people do. But they did get better once I got pregnant."

"So you're saying it's gonna hurt really bad until I have a baby?"

"No, Laura. I don't know what yours are going to be like. What I am saying is that you can trust God."

"Okay. It's just ... it's kinda scary."

"I know, Laura. I was scared too. Your grandma didn't even talk to me. She gave me a book and some pads the first time I started. I was terrified."

"Are you serious? That's crazy!"

"Your grandmother has many good qualities. But being direct isn't one of them."

"Well, how did you get so direct then?"

"I wasn't always. Your dad helped me a lot with that. He taught me that it was important to deal with things and not ignore them."

"Um, Mom? Does Dad know about, you know, all of this stuff too?"

"He does, Laura. He and I talked about it yesterday, and decided it was time to talk to you."

"Okay. Are you … are you going to help me when it happens? I mean, just like the first time?"

"Of course, Laura. That's what I'm here for. I love you! Let's pray about this, okay?"

15

Conversation about Masturbation

Conversation between Dad and 15-year-old Son, Sean

These types of conversations have been going on for several years.

"Sean, did you get my email about tonight?"

"What email?

"Sean."

"Yeah, Dad I got it. I'm here. It's cool."

"Okay, great. We have some new ground to cover."

"How could there possibly be anything you haven't covered yet?"

"Well, I've covered almost everything. I have been being a bit of a chicken with this last topic."

"Chicken?"

"Well, yeah, I have. We need to talk about masturbation."

"Wow, Dad! Stop. I get it. I don't think we need to go in depth here, okay?"

"Yes, Sean we have to. And, I'm sorry I have taken so long to get to this issue."

"Okay, it's cool. Don't worry about it. Can I go now?"

"I am afraid not. This is one of the problems that people don't talk much about except to make jokes about it."

"Yeah, I guess. It's pretty much a constant on Xbox Live."

"It doesn't just happen online. Older men joke about it too.

"Are you serious? Guys still do that, even at your age?"

"Uh, yes, sometimes even guys older than me."

"Gross, Dad."

"All right, be serious. You remember the two most important things about sex and marriage?"

"Um, that would be God designed sex for marriage and sex and stuff should always honor God ... oh, and like our thoughts and when we have sex is only for the person that you marry. So that's like three things, right?"

"Right, great! Okay, I am trying to keep this short and not too heavy, just so you know."

"The shorter the better."

"Sean, do you remember when we talked about being respectful, and a wise son listening to his father's counsel?"

"Yeah, from Proverbs. Sorry."

"That's okay. Now, given how well you just explained what things are important, how do you think masturbation fits into that picture?"

"Um ... I guess it doesn't?"

"Sean, I am not looking for the 'right' answer. I want to know what you really think."

"That is what I think. I mean ... I guess it's like you said before, sex is all about serving just your wife, I guess, and, you know, the other thing is just about my—uh—yourself."

"That's very true, Sean."

"But, I was talking with my friend Paul and he said that at his school he had a class where they said that it's not bad, it's natural and everybody does it and it is just super-strict Christians who are all messed about it."

"And what did you think of that, the natural part?"

"I mean, we already talked about it. It makes sense. Natural is not always good, right?"

"Yes, outstanding! Masturbation is obviously something one person does alone. And that does not fit with what the Bible says about sexual relations. That is what I am trying to get across. When people do things that don't follow God's direction, things don't turn out well."

"Like?"

"I have a good friend who does biblical counseling, you know him, Scott ..."

"Oh, yeah."

"Well, he counsels a lot of families where masturbation is a problem. He says three things usually happen when a teenager, or anybody really, gets involved with masturbation. There is doubt, then guilt and then kids become slaves to it."

"Uh, yeah, I can kinda see that ... he say anything else?"

"He really made a really big deal that parents can't get upset with their kids if this is going on. Being angry,

hurt and offended, which is what most parents do, doesn't help anything. He said kids just have to start rethinking things differently and trust God to help them see how unhelpful masturbation really is."

"Um ... "

"Look, Sean, we are about out of time tonight. So we will pick it up next week, okay. Thanks for hanging in there tonight. I love you, son."

"Hey, Dad, thanks."

"No problem."